CW01424925

IF YOU'VE FORGOTTEN
THE NAMES OF THE CLOUDS,
YOU'VE LOST YOUR WAY

AN
INTRODUCTION
TO AMERICAN INDIAN
THOUGHT & PHILOSOPHY

IF YOU'VE FORGOTTEN THE NAMES OF THE CLOUDS, YOU'VE LOST YOUR WAY

AN
INTRODUCTION
TO AMERICAN INDIAN
THOUGHT & PHILOSOPHY

Russell Means & Bayard Johnson

Copyright © 2012 by Russell Means and Bayard Johnson
All Rights Reserved
First Printed Edition
First Printing 2013

Published by Treaty Publications
Porcupine South Dakota and Santa Monica California

Address all inquiries to:
Treaty Publications
P.O. Box 99
Porcupine, SD 57772

IF YOU'VE FORGOTTEN THE NAMES OF THE CLOUDS,
YOU'VE LOST YOUR WAY:
An Introduction to American Indian Thought and Philosophy
Russell Means, Bayard Johnson

ISBN-13: 978-1482068108
ISBN-10: 1482068109

Produced and printed in the United States of America

dedicated to

the unborn and future generations

CONTENTS

FOREWORD

The reason we decided to write this book is because The Trickster has completely tricked my people. The Trickster, or Iktomi, has come into our land, and completely colonized the Lakotah Nation. In February of this year I cut my hair in mourning. This was for my own people, who are dead, and are only play-acting at being Indians. Only a few even realize that they are colonized. The Heyoka, the one who lives backwards, has come into our land to try to get the people out of this death condition, but it's not working—the people are not listening. They're not learning.

My Great-Grandma Aggie, my Grandma Twinklestar, my Auntie Faith, my Mother, my Grandpa John Feather, and many others too numerous to name, all taught me many many things. What they didn't teach me was that as the oldest brother, I was supposed to pass this knowledge down to my younger brothers. I didn't do it because I didn't know. Not until I joined the American Indian Movement, AIM, did I realize this.

When I joined AIM was when I met the old people— those who were born in the latter part of the 1800s, had never been to school, and were raised by people who were born free. There was Pete Catches, Frank Fools Crow, Frank Kills Enemy, Henry Crow Dog, John Fire, Severt Young Bear Sr., Sally Red Owl, Mrs. Janis, and many old ladies on Rosebud and Pine Ridge whose names I never knew. They taught me and counseled me, all of them. They would all visit me, and I would visit them.

So this book is about what I learned from these old

people. This book is an introduction—a very sketchy introduction—to Matriarchy. The Indian way of life is very misunderstood, and has almost disappeared from the Earth.

This book is a partial collection of everything I've come to know from my people—from my ancestors, from people who were born free, from my relatives, and from my own experiences...as well as from other Indian Nations in the Western Hemisphere who all shared the same world view.

THE ANCESTORS

Every part of this Earth is sacred to my people. Every hillside, every valley, every plain and grove... the very dust upon which you now stand responds more lovingly to our footsteps than to yours, because it is rich with the blood of our ancestors...

Seattle, Suquamish, mid 1800s

Come with us now on a journey to another world...the way it was everywhere on Earth, when people all across the globe lived in paradise. Today, only in scattered locations, in small shrinking pockets and forgotten remote islands and mountains and jungles, does this paradise still exist.

To understand the American Indians, or any indigenous people, it is essential to start with the Ancestors. Our Ancestors are vital to the Indian world-view, and are held in as high regard as if they were alive today, and walking among us.

Our Ancestors are our constant witness and companion. They know everything. They are part of us, as we are part of them. In this way, an American Indian is never a solitary or lonely individual. Existential angst is unknown. We know who we are and we are never alone. We are part of something greater than ourselves.

This makes us responsible. An entire family or clan is responsible for any act of violence of any of its members, not only in the present and the past, but even into the future. Honor is not purely individual, it exists among individuals of course, but it also incorporates our immediate families, our clans, the Ancestors, and extends out to include the entire Universe.

An American Indian is aware that if disgrace or dishonor is brought upon oneself, then our Grandmother Earth has been insulted as well. These beliefs and principles are real. They are based on the clear and obvious connection between ourselves and the natural world that nurtures and supports us in every moment of our existence. Our connection to the Ancestors guides our actions in every situation.

LANGUAGES OF THE NEW WORLD

How smooth must be the language of the whites, when they can make right look like wrong, and wrong like right.

Black Hawk, Sauk, early 1800s

Conversation was never begun at once, nor in a hurried manner. No one was quick with a question, no matter how important, and no one was pressed for an answer. A pause giving time for thought was the truly courteous way of beginning and conducting a conversation. Silence was meaningful with the Lakotah, and his granting a space of silence to the speech-maker and his own moment of silence before talking was done in the practice of true politeness and regard for the rule that, "thought comes before speech."

Luther Standing Bear, Oglala Lakotah, early 1900s

This book is an attempt at explaining a very complex world view and a complete set of life ways—that there are no negatives in the Matriarchal world view. This truth is demonstrated in our languages.

The very essence of being an American Indian is expressed in our languages. They are unlike the languages of the "Old World," which are combinations of older languages and are traceable to the same few mother tongues. Languages all over the "Old World" have been written down for centuries, unlike our languages which have remained free until recent times.

Once a language is written down, its speakers suffer

immediate consequences. One of the first casualties is memory—as soon as you can write something down, the power to remember goes quickly. Also lost is much of the richness and expressiveness of language.

If you look at the earliest written versions of *Beowulf*, transcribed from the spoken word of the minstrel, a traveling story-teller, you see use of startling, almost magical imagery. Beowulf and friends "traveled the whale-road," they "oar-dipped across the roof of the fishes." These words make pictures, evoking the myriad life around them, the searing richness of experience...all this was soon sacrificed for efficiency. The spoken word is the realm of storytellers, poets, and visionaries, it is a plastic and infinitely expandable medium, an art form. Written language crosses into the domain of word-accountants, "experts" who spend their lives compiling catalogues of words, immense dictionaries trying to affix an exact, almost numerical value to every utterance and human emotion. Certainly this can be a fascinating pursuit, but it's the antithesis of creative process, which is what speaking in a free language used to be all about.

Ironically, not only does creativity and expressiveness suffer once a language becomes a written language—it also becomes easier to lie. When a story or account is written down, history for example, it becomes the accepted version of truth no matter how false the information, or how biased the source. People who live in the oral tradition, however, have to be able to remember what they said. The only way to be sure of this is to tell the truth. Liars are frequently found out because their stories are inconsistent—when they're not drawing on truthful memories, they frequently can't remember what they said. The stories of liars become inconsistent with the accounts of others. Lying just doesn't work when you're face to face in the oral tradition. Writers, working alone, sometimes under a pseudonym, or even anonymously, are not really accountable. They can write anything they want without regard to fairness or truth.

The languages of the American Indians who never

bothered with writing have extremely descriptive words and expressions for natural phenomena, and are entirely missing words for things that don't exist in our culture — things like murder, deceit, and lying. How could anyone lie when the Ancestors are continually bearing witness?When not only yourself but everything you love would be dishonored? Dishonored not by getting caught in a lie, but by the very telling of it. We had no use for written language until our tongues were stolen from us by kidnapping our children into English-only boarding schools, and many of our languages were in danger of completely dying out.

Because our languages are connected to the way we think and view the world, to who we are, we lose our way of life when we lose our language. The Lakotah language is on the cusp of extinction. Therefore the Lakotah people are on the cusp of extinction.

In the Lakotah language, the language of the central plains of North America, there are 52 different kinds of clouds that we have names for. With that knowledge and wisdom, by recognizing the often subtle differences between types of clouds and their characteristics, we can accurately predict the weather up to two days and nights in advance. Hence the name of our book, "*If You've Forgotten the Names of the Clouds, You've Lost Your Way.*"

Our language is equally rich and expressive in its description of all the natural phenomena that surrounds us. The winds that blow across the plains, the snow that covers us in winter. We understand, like all indigenous people, that we are intrinsically part of a system that is not above or outside or separate from the natural world and natural law, we are part of a mosaic or web of life.

Indians never try to explain the unknown. Think about it, what kind of fool would try to explain the unknown — after all, it's unknown. That's why you hear us talk about the Great Mystery, which we treat with great respect. We don't call the Great Mystery by familiar names which we made up, and draw pictures wherein "He" invariably looks like older and wiser and less obese versions of ourselves. We always thought the white man was foolish because he claims to know everything about the unknown while knowing nothing about this life; in contrast, we Indians know everything about this life and nothing about what comes after...we and the Patriarch are opposites, and never the twain shall meet...

How many words in the English language can be used to describe the clouds? Certainly fewer than 52. In English, by contrast, there are numerous words for killing—murder, slaughter, torture, evisceration, disembowelment, decapitation, strangulation, genocide, patricide, fratricide, matricide—the list goes on and on. These are words that never existed in our language, words for concepts that never existed in our world, before the white man.

How rich are English and the other European tongues, compared to languages of the Western Hemisphere and other indigenous societies, in terms of connecting with and understanding the natural world, and Natural Law?

Back in the 1970s, we began to see clouds never seen before on the High Plains. Back in the winter of 1974, Severt Young Bear Sr., a Lakotah Elder born in the 1800s, said that the Zodiac, or Star System, as we call it, was also changing. But for that to be explained, you would have to consult with someone with Lakotah star knowledge.

MATRIARCHAL TIME

The Universe, which controls all life, has a female and male balance that is prevalent throughout our Sacred Grandmother, the Earth. This balance has to be acknowledged and become the determining factor in all of one's decisions, be they spiritual, social, healthful, educational or economic. Once the balance has become an integral part of one's life, all planning, research, direct action and follow-up becomes a matter of course. The goals that were targeted become a reality on a consistent basis. Good things happen to good People; remember, time is on our side.

Russell Means

Our time is based on Matriarchal or Lunar time—the entire Universe, all the stars in the Heavens, rotate on a cycle of 280 days. This also happens to be the gestation time of the human female. This is the basis for the Aztec Calendar, and the Mayan Calendar.

The growing hysteria during the build-up to the year 2012 has been an amusing phenomenon. According to Mayans, who are most familiar with their own calendar, the paradigm shift associated with 2012, or the "end of the world" scenario envisioned by many whites, would not actually arrive in the year 2012 of the Christian calendar. When a year is calculated at 280 days, by Matriarchal time, the Mayans tell us that the year 2012 actually already came and went, long ago—over 500 years ago in fact, in 1492. There's your paradigm shift and the end of the world all rolled up in one.

The 2012 phenomenon which is agitating people these

days is really about something else. A window that is now open and that has been open is closing. Now is a time of exaggeration and acceleration, a cycle is ending, the Earth is tired and needs rest...

Indians believe there have been four cycles for the human. Christians and Jews and Muslims believe in two cycles (before and after the flood). In each of these cycles, after the humans failed, there followed a time of purification when only a few survived. We are now nearing the end of the 4th cycle. And once again, humans are failing—will we survive? All religions seem to agree we are heading for another cleansing. Is Grandmother Earth finally tiring of the two-leggeds, the only species on Earth that is far out of balance?

LAKOTAH MORNING THANK-YOU PRAYER

O holy Great Mystery, thank you for this day.

I thank you for the Universe, which is our tabernacle, our house of worship.

Thank you for the Star People, who watch over our water and all that lives, and give us direction and a place in life.

Thank you for the Moon, which also watches over the water and purifies the women naturally.

Thank you for the water.

Thank you for our sacred Grandmother, the Earth, mother of all living beings, for they are our relatives.

Thank you for the East Wind, which brings the Morning Star which gives us the dawn of a new day, so that we will not repeat the mistakes of yesterday. The East Wind brings a newness into our hearts, minds, bodies and spirits, renewing the spirits of our sacred Grandmother, the Earth and of all our relatives.

And thank you for the Black Tail Deer People, who live in the East and watch over us.

Thank you for the South Wind, which brings warmth and generosity to our hearts, minds, bodies and spirits, as well as to our sacred Grandmother, the Earth, and to all our relatives.

And thank you for the Owl People, who live in the South and watch over us.

Thank you for the West Wind, which gives us the lightning and thunder spirits, which bring the cleansing and refreshing rains for our sacred Grandmother, the Earth, and all our relatives, and which brings cleanliness and refreshment to our hearts, minds, bodies and spirits.

And thank you for the Buffalo People, who live in the West and watch over us.

Thank you for the North Wind, which brings strong and enduring winds that give our sacred Grandmother, the Earth, and all our relatives strength and endurance, and brings strength and endurance to our hearts, minds, bodies and spirits.

And thank you for the Elk People, who live in the North, and watch over us.

Thank you for all the winged beings of the air for their teachings, their generosity and their sacrifices. Thank you especially for the eagle, who flies the highest, sees the furthest, and is faithful to its mate.

Thank you for the four-leggeds, who give us so much and teach us so much, for their sacrifices and sharing.

And thank you especially for the buffalo, because as the buffalo goes, so go our people.

Thank you for all our relatives who crawl and swim and live within the earth, for their sacrifices and sharing and their generosity.

Thank you for all their teachings and for everything that they give us.

Thank you also for all the green, growing things of the Earth. They teach us so much and give us so much. Thank you for their sacrifices and for their sharing.

Thank you especially for the tree with the whispering leaves, for its strength and independence and its teachings. And thank you for the sacred Tree of Live, which we must nourish and care for to ensure that it blossoms once again, allowing our people to live as they were intended.

Thank you for the salmon and the other fishes, who teach that it is our birthright to return to our home.

Thank you for the spider, who teaches us the foibles of life in the guise of Iktomi, the Trickster.

Thank you for each of the sacred ceremonies brought us by the holy White Buffalo Calf Woman.

Thank you for our purification lodge, which enlightens us with understanding of purification and cleanliness.

Thank you for the Sundance, which allows men an opportunity to comprehend the miracle of new life by sharing, in a small way, the experience of childbirth.

Thank you for the Crying for a Vision Ceremony, which permits us to recognize a positive and independent road to follow throughout life.

Thank you for the Making of Relatives Ceremony, which allows us to bring new citizens into our nation, our family, our clan.

Thank you for the Keeping of the Spirit Ceremony, which allows us the privilege of showing respect for our ancestors, and brings the community together to share and celebrate the deeds of the departed.

Thank you for the Throwing of the Ball Ceremony, which brings the community together as one heart, one mind, one spirit, one body.

Thank you for the Making of Woman Ceremony that allows girls and young women to aspire to being worthy of the universe.

Thank you for the healing ceremonies and sweet medicines produced by our green relatives who grow. Together they care for the infirm, the crippled and the sick.

Thank you for the soil, for the clouds, for the white blanket that comes to cover our Grandmother, the Earth, in the time of cold.

Thank you for the sacred colors, together representing everything that is worthy in life, and individually teaching us so much.

Thank you for the wind that travels in a circle, for it teaches us respect and wonder and awe.

I thank you for everything that is holy and sacred and good. We are all related.

Lakotah Morning Prayer

In traditional Lakotah society, the husband wakes at first light, in the early pre-dawn. He doesn't speak, he doesn't wake his wife sleeping beside him. He goes outside, alone, and speaks the Lakotah Morning Prayer with the Morning Star when it is the only star left in the dawn sky. Speaking the Morning Prayer clears the mind of all worries and anxiety, and makes a person aware of his place in the mosaic of life. It humbles you.

Ready to start the day, the husband turns back inside the Tipi, and goes and combs his wife's hair. Neither one speaks a word. The husband's first interaction of the day with his wife is a very sacred exchange. Hair is very important as it grows from the head, where the brain resides. Hair holds memory. It is only cut when one is in mourning. This first exchange between husband and wife is a caressing touch, on a sacred part of the body.

THE TIPI

I am going to venture that the man who sat on the ground in his tipi meditating on life and its meaning, accepting the kinship of all creatures, and acknowledging unity with the universe of things, was infusing into his being the true essence of civilization.
Luther Standing Bear, Oglala Lakotah, early 1900s

The Tipi is much more than just a mobile home. The Tipi is a daily reminder of life. Tipi means "clean house."

The Tipi represents a woman. The two poles which attach to the flaps, and which allow the flaps to be opened and closed — those poles are her arms.

Of course all of our homes face East, toward the Morning Star. At night, you close the poles and the flaps fold over, like a woman's arms, wrapped around her. Coming into the Tipi is like entering her womb. The entrance is round, like everything holy. You have to bend over to enter or leave, making you humble.

In the morning you open the flaps, and fresh air comes in, and the stale air goes out, just like a woman's cleansing cycle. The poles that support the Tipi represent the men — when you see them wrapped together, standing in unity, only the strongest wind, a tornado, can dislodge them and upset the home. Look how many men it takes to support a woman. And every man is the son of a woman, he comes from a woman, and is part of her. Connected, united, mutually supportive.

Architects the world over have ascertained that the Tipi is the finest mobile home ever devised. A Tipi can withstand higher winds than a dome or any other shape. Due to the Tipi's conical design, an increase in wind causes stronger down-force on the poles, making the Tipi free of the need for a foundation, and making it grip the Earth more securely as the weather gets stormier.

So in many ways the Tipi constantly reminds us of life, and of the Woman's exalted place in the world. Females live longer, have more strength and stamina, and can stand more pain than males. The Tipi is a daily teaching that kids grow up with. Their home is a female that is supported by men, and it cannot be destroyed when the community stands in unity.

NATURAL LAW

"Why will you take by force what you may obtain by love? Why will you destroy us who supply you with food? What can you get by war?... We are unarmed, and willing to give you what you ask, if you come in a friendly manner..."
Powhatan, Algonquin Confederacy, to John Smith, 1609

From the Matriarchal perspective, the world is a nurturing place. A place where gifts are freely given. When the Spanish and Portuguese Conquistadores arrived, the Aztecs and the Incas couldn't understand why these newcomers were so crazed with greed for things like gold. All they had to do was ask, and the Indians would've given it to them.

Columbus, upon his first contact with Indians of the Caribbean, wrote that the natives were so generous and peaceful as to be a fault. A fault?? Generosity and peacefulness a fault? What kind of world do you suppose he was coming from? The world of the Inquisition. The Dark Ages. The Black Death. The American Indians would become all too familiar with this world, very soon.

If you live in a world where everything you need is freely available, greed looks like a form of insanity. Why would anyone want more than they need? The Earth provides an unlimited supply. Just as a Mother provides her child with every possible need, the Earth does the same for all her children, humans along with all other creatures. If you follow Natural Law you're not afraid of death. You see the natural cycles of death and rebirth all around you, in your parents and your children, in winter's dormancy and the new leaves of spring, the regeneration of every kind of new life. Indigenous old people do not cling to life, they are not fearful, when they are burdens to their societies they simply leave. In every cycle of nature through their entire lives they have observed rebirth, reincarnation—death and decay transformed into new life—and they know that we are all part of this cycle.

Specific details of how this cycle operates are not important. Indigenous people don't lie and make things up when they don't know the complete answer. They don't pretend or claim to know things they have no way of knowing. They don't write down the ravings of those hearing voices and claim that these are the words of some 'god'...because life is lived in balance, language develops with no negatives, only positives. There is no word for lying, in the Lakotah language one is incapable of insulting anyone or anything. In Natural Law there is a place for everything— where is the evil? There is no evil in nature. Living by Natural Law, we perceive fully through the senses, we develop a full and rich appreciation for the real world around us, for what we experience in everyday life. For reality.

THE NATURAL PURITY OF WOMEN

Women live longer than men. They are purified naturally, in rhythm with the moon. The longevity of women is one of the reasons our Clan system is based on women. When men leave this life, we want our women and children to be comfortable and secure within a social structure made up of her relatives and friends. This is all consistent with Natural Law, which guides us in everything we do and believe. Natural Law encompasses all of life, and it is our teacher.

Russell Means

In Patriarchy they domesticated the dog, taking all its natural sense away. In the same way the Patriarch has denigrated the Woman, by calling her a bitch. That is, a dog that will mate with any male dog, over and over again, as long as they're in heat. Among wolves or coyotes, never domesticated, only the alpha female mates, and only with the alpha male. The other females take on the role of aunties. Every individual has a place, according to Natural Law.

Women are purified monthly, every 28 days, usually over four days. Twenty-eight is the number of ribs of the buffalo. There are 28 days between full moons. So we see that women are in balance with the Universe.

When women live together, their purification cycle gets in tune with one another, so they all have their cycle at the same time. When you live in a small village, all the women get in tune with the Universe as manifested by the full moon. So when the full moon comes, all the women would remove themselves to what today is commonly referred to as the Moon Lodge, for their purification cycle. The young girls, age 9 to11 or 12, who are about to become women themselves, wait on their elders, cooking their food, and serving them. Everyone in the community understands what is happening during this time, as the women remove themselves from the men and the young children.

Europe originally followed this practice in pre-Christian times, when the people of Europe were indigenous. When the Romans arrived, they disrupted this custom. The Roman Catholic priests convinced the men that the women were conspiring to rob them of their power, brewing witches' spells, and they introduced Halloween as an anti-woman holiday. Millions of women were burned as witches in the brutal process of replacing Matriarchy with Patriarchy, making man all-powerful and turning the indigenous world upside-down.

FINDING BALANCE IN THE INIPI

The wise man believes profoundly in silence – the sign of perfect equilibrium. Silence is the absolute poise or balance of body, mind and spirit. The man who preserves his selfhood ever calm and unshaken by the storms of existence – not a leaf astir on the tree, not a ripple upon the surface of the shining pool – his is the ideal attitude and conduct of life. Silence is the cornerstone of character.
Ohiyesa, Wahpeton Santee Lakotah, early 1900s

The Inipi is a way that the men of indigenous North America have devised to get in balance with the female. The Inipi was devised to give men some idea what it was like to be purified from within.

The men found it necessary to do this more often than the women, going to the Inipi every few days. It used to be a violation of Christian Law to bathe, and when the white man saw us bathing and cleansing ourselves in the steam bath or Inipi, they claimed this was proof that we were pagans and heathens. The Jesuits and Christian ministers wrote back to Europe about these heathens who were bathing all the time, in violation of Christian principles and church law. For several hundred years, church law forbade bathing because it required nudity, which was a condition which led to Original Sin. This is how the Europeans created plagues and epidemic diseases – from a condition of almost unimaginable filth.

The Inipi is constructed as a small lodge with a single doorway, dome-shaped, which represents the womb. Men enter the Inipi naked, the same way they emerged from the womb, with their hair down and loose.

A Fireman and his Assistant heat rocks on an open fire outside the Inipi, then bring them inside and place them in a pit dug in the center. Water is thrown on the rocks, creating steam. It can become extremely hot, and the door is opened a minimum of four times, for ventilation. If it gets too hot for any of the men inside, they say "We are all related," and the door is opened to let steam escape. The men sing, talk, tell jokes, pray. Healing of all kinds takes place in the Inipi— psychological and physical.

SUNDANCE

To Make Medicine is to engage upon a special period of fasting, thanksgiving, prayer and self-denial, even of self-torture. The procedure is entirely a devotional exercise. The purpose is to subdue the passions of the flesh and to improve the spiritual self. The bodily abstinence and the mental concentration upon lofty thoughts cleanses both the body and the soul and puts them into or keeps them in health. Then the individual mind gets closer toward conformity with the mind of the Great Medicine above us.

Wooden Leg, Cheyenne, late 1800s

The Sundance, which is performed only by the men, is a celebration of Childbirth. Women sacrifice their own flesh and blood to create life. Men can only sacrifice a little flesh and blood, obviously we can't create life. But in order to have some understanding of what a woman experiences, to get a little peek into this experience, we do our 4 days of dancing, of suffering, and then our meager little piercing of flesh.

The Sundance is traditionally done in the spring, always in the mountains. All religions know, even patriarchal ones, that the higher you go in the mountains, the clearer the mind becomes. Western science attributes this to an increase in ions at higher elevations.

In the Lakotah way, the Tree of Life is the Aspen tree—the anarchist of the tree world, which grows anywhere and everywhere it wants to in the mountains, growing in families and nations. A young girl helps the men who are running the Sundance to select an aspen tree, which is carried by the men to the area where the Sundance will take place. The sacred colors are tied to the branches of the tree, along with the ropes which will be used for piercing toward the conclusion of the Sundance. A hole is dug, the tree is erected, and there is a celebration and Last Feast, because the dancers are about to commence a fast of four nights and four days.

These four days represent the tribulations that women go through during childbirth. The medical reason for the four-day fast is that the blood will withdraw from the capillaries and the surface of the skin. This way, after the fourth day, when our skin is pierced by very sharp knives, and a rope is tied through the loop of flesh, there is very little bleeding, just a trickle.

This ripping of the flesh represents childbirth. This is only a meager way to attempt to approximate what every woman experiences in creating life. All the songs that are sung are prayer songs.

We are allowed no water and no food, even during the occasional breaks for rest. The prayer songs are what you dance to all day long. There are more than two dozen prayer songs, Sundance songs, and they all mean a specific thing that you pray for.

While the overriding reason for the Sundance is to get in balance with the Female, you can also Sundance for many other reasons—for the village, for an individual, for the nation, or for any particular purpose. On the fourth day, after ripping free the flesh, we are then allowed to feast. At all times during the Sundance, we are communing with the Great Mystery.

People also get doctored at the Sundance. You bring a pipe full of tobacco and you smoke it with the man who runs the Sundance. There are medicine people there at the Sundance who will doctor you, and heal many different kinds of ailments.

The Sundance has changed since the time a few generations back when we were free, but the principle remains the same. Originally the entire process took 12 days—four days of preparation, four days of dancing, four days for the Feast, Giveaway and recovery. Nowadays people have time constraints.

The Sundance was outlawed by the U.S. government in the late 19th century—so much for your freedom of religion—and was revived during the 1960s. Unfortunately, some perverse practices have crept into some imperfect versions of the Sundance that are put on by quacks and charlatans. Some Sundances even include women as Sundancers! Boy are they missing the point.

To be complete, a man might do the Sundance as many as 20 different times. The feeling of connection with Spiritual

Power at the conclusion of the Sundance is unlike any other experience in a man's life. Perhaps, in some infinitesimal way, it begins to approach the feeling a woman has upon giving birth.

THE MAKING OF A WOMAN CEREMONY

Wakan Tanka, Great Mystery, teach me how to trust my heart, my mind, my intuition, my inner knowing, the senses of my body, the blessings of my spirit. Teach me to trust these things so that I may enter my Sacred Space and love beyond my fear, and thus walk in balance with the passing of each glorious Sun.

Lakotah Prayer

Among the Lakotah, Dakota and Nakota, we have Seven Sacred Ceremonies brought to us by our spiritual teacher. All seven involve the Sacred Pipe, which the white man calls the peace pipe. The Sundance and the Inipi are two of these ceremonies.

Another is the Making of a Woman Ceremony, which is of course when a girl changes from a child into a woman. As this profound transformation takes place, the developing Woman is taken into a Tipi for four days and four nights, where she is instructed and advised by the older women of the community. This is not a shameful or embarrassing or humiliating or degrading episode in a young woman's life, as in many patriarchal cultures which honor the male and denigrate the female.

The Making of a Woman Ceremony ensures that a girl fully understands what she is going through physically, socially, emotionally, reproductively, sexually...and these lessons are learned in a reverent and joyous atmosphere of celebration, great respect and honor. There is no shame in nature, and in living by Natural Law. Only dignity.

CRYING FOR A VISION CEREMONY

A very great vision is needed and the man who has it must follow it as the Eagle seeks the deepest blue of the sky.
                                    Crazy Horse, Oglala Lakotah, 1800s

We have the Crying For A Vision Ceremony among young men, when we go into the mountains, and literally cry for a vision. The young man must get himself to the place where he is this serious and committed to receiving the vision that will guide him in his life. Usually this Vision Quest, as it is sometimes called, continues for four days and four nights. The young man is without food and water, and is naked except for a buffalo robe.

If a vision comes partway through the four days and nights, you must guard against the Iktomi (the Trickster) and the possibility of a false vision. This happened to me one time. Around Day Two, a fly came buzzing up and landed nearby, and said to me, "All right, here I am—you've had your vision and you can go down now." I was happily packing up my buffalo robe when I suddenly realized, Wait a second, I'm going to go down there and they'll ask me about my vision, and I'll have to say, "My protector is a *fly*..?!" So I stayed until receiving a true vision.

On the fourth day, in the morning, I knew my people would be coming soon to take me down off the mountain. As I sat naked on the buffalo robe, looking down at the Sacred Pipe that I was holding, I heard something moving on my left, to the North. I looked toward the sound, and saw running away from me, in the middle of a clearing, a pronghorn antelope of huge size, as big as a horse. Pronghorn antelopes are very small, frail creatures, so I knew what I saw was sacred and holy. I watched until it disappeared into the woods farther down the mountain.

As I once again looked down at the Pipe, and contemplated what I had witnessed, I heard a grunt. Directly in front of me, to the East, stood a huge black buffalo, staring at me and pawing the Earth with his front hoof, on the North side of him. I knew I was in his territory, and I began to feel butterflies in the pit of my stomach. At first I thought this was fear. As I looked at him, I realized he was too huge to be natural, and I began to cry. I looked down at my Pipe and began praying really hard. A noise made me look up again, and I saw the huge buffalo heading West on the North side of me. He left the clearing and entered the woods, heading down toward where we were camped on the plains.

My son Scott, twelve years of age at the time, had gone up with me to also cry for a vision, for two days and nights. Scott was back down in camp by this time. He saw the big black buffalo come out of the woods halfway down the mountain, and then disappear while still in plain sight.

Meanwhile, I was still on the mountain, contemplating this vision I'd just had. Later, after being brought down from the mountaintop, the Holy Man who had put me up there took Scott, myself and others into the Purification Lodge. There I came to understand the beginnings of the interpretation of my vision. And as I grew older, the full meanings would come to me.

THE THROWING OF THE BALL CEREMONY

I have seen that in any great undertaking it is not enough for a man to depend simply upon himself.
                              Lone Man, Teton Lakotah, late 1800s

The Throwing of the Ball Ceremony is an event which draws the entire community together, spiritually. The main purpose of the ceremony is to teach responsibility – spiritually, socially, interpersonally. This ceremony helps to bond the community into a cohesive unit.

In essence, indigenous society is anarchistic, centered around not any kind of governmental or political institutions, but rather based on the family. The only structure imposed on indigenous societies in terms of schedule or calendar is the one that occurs naturally – the order of the seasons of the year.

The Throwing of the Ball Ceremony can be initiated by any adult in the village, and could happen at any time of the year. As a spiritual ceremony, it is done with great reverence. A ball is made of different kinds of hides wrapped together, and to the accompaniment of specific songs, the ball is first thrown by a respected local leader, either female or male. The entire community is present, and the leaders of the village's various societies or clans designate who will be in position to catch the ball when it is thrown.

Each time the ball is thrown, the one who catches the ball is expected to say good things about everyone out there, and they also express thanks and appreciation to everyone present, to every member of the village. Then it is the recipient's turn to throw the ball, after which they remove themself to the sidelines.

This process continues until everyone has had their turn to catch the ball, and to speak praises of all who share their community. Clearly, this invariably creates great harmony among the community, because everyone is required to search in their heart and find good things to say about everyone else — even those they may have experienced conflict or tension with in the past.

Unity among the community is strengthened, underappreciated qualities brought to the fore, respect and honor are emphasized, and positive feelings and truths for one another encouraged. Negativity dissipates.

THE KEEPING OF THE SPIRIT CEREMONY

To us the ashes of our ancestors are sacred and their resting place is hallowed ground... Your dead cease to love you and the land of their birth as soon as they pass the portals of the tomb and wander way beyond the stars. They are soon forgotten and never return. Our dead never forget the beautiful world that gave them being...
Seattle, Suquamish, mid 1800s

The Keeping of the Spirit Ceremony allows grief to be expressed in a healthy way, while honoring the departed.

The Releasing of the Spirit Ceremony occurs a year after someone dies. An altar of sorts is built, and for an entire year people bring gifts and leave them at the altar to honor the deceased. After a year all those gifts are re-distributed.

This ceremony both honors the dead, while also serving as a reminder to those that remain that material objects belong to the realm of the living. Wealth is equalized so that nobody becomes too rich and so that those in material need get some help. It is important to note that these gifts are received honorably, with dignity, as they are a measure of the respect expressed for the one who has passed, and who has now graduated from this world into the position of those most highly regarded in indigenous society — the Ancestors.

WHITE BUFFALO CALF WOMAN

When I was a young man I went to a medicine man for advice concerning my future. The medicine man said, "I have not much to tell you except to help you understand this Earth on which you live. If a man is to succeed...he must not be governed by his inclination, but by an understanding of the ways of animals and of his natural surroundings, gained through close observation. The Earth is large, and on it live many animals. The Earth is under the protection of something which at times becomes visible to the eye."
Lone Man, Teton Lakotah, late 1800s

All these ceremonies were brought to us by the White Buffalo Calf Woman. Our spirituality was brought to us by a woman, via an animal.

This is the way it happened. Two men, while hunting, saw a white buffalo calf coming toward them. This was very unusual, so they knew something momentous was likely to happen. They watched closely as a cloud of dust enveloped the buffalo calf. When the dust cleared, the two hunters saw a very beautiful young woman in the place where the white buffalo calf had stood a moment before. Right away, one of the men had sexual thoughts about the woman, and—poof! He turned to dust.

The other hunter stood watching in awe as the White Buffalo Calf Woman approached and presented him with a pipe, along with instructions for three sacred ceremonies. These first three were The Making of a Woman Ceremony, the Inipi, and the Sundance. She told him how to use the pipe in ceremony, and advised him that the pipe was to be cared for by a woman. She also informed him that she would return at a later time with instructions for more Sacred Ceremonies, as needed. Turning to leave, the White Buffalo Calf Woman transformed back into a white buffalo calf.

The Hunter went back to his village, where he gave the Sacred Pipe to an Elder Woman. It has been kept safely among the Lakotah people ever since, passed on from generation to generation, always in the care of a highly honored and respected Elder Woman.

The indigenous male is always seeking to get in balance with the female. Always seeking some insight into the experience of the female and her unique position as a creator of life. Men of the Lakotah Nation have always felt great affection, honor and gratitude toward the White Buffalo Calf Woman for giving them the Inipi and the Sundance—two of the first three Sacred Ceremonies given to humankind—for the specific purpose of helping the men develop and strengthen this sacred bond with our Mother the Universe.

MARRIAGE

Oh Great Spirit whose voice I hear in the Winds and whose breath gives life to all the World, Hear me! I am small and weak, I need your strength and wisdom, let me walk in beauty, and let my eyes ever behold the red and purple sunset. Make my hands respect the things you have made, and make my ears sharp to hear your voice. Make me wise so I may see ever so clearly the ways you have to teach me. Let me learn the lessons you have hidden in every leaf and cloud. I seek your strength, not to be greater than my brother, but to fight my greatest enemy...myself. Make me always ready to come to you with clean hands and straight eyes, so that when life fades, as the fading sunset, my Spirit may come to you without shame.

Chief Yellow Lark, Lakotah, late 1800s

Before a man is in a position to get married, he should be well on his way to being established in the world. By his late 20s or early 30s, a man will be successful in life, making himself attractive to a prospective wife. Her family would not have to worry about their daughter and their grandchildren being well-taken care of, because the suitor has already proven that he can make it in the world and has the resources to care for a family.

The ideal age for childbearing for a woman is mid-teens to the mid-twenties, when she is physically strongest and most fertile. When having a child, it's important to impart to the child all possible strength from the mother. If she marries and has children beginning at 15 or 16, a woman can have two children spaced six years apart, and her second child will reach the age of six when the mother is still in her twenties. In addition to being at the peak of her youth and fertility while giving birth to her children, the mother will also have plenty of strength and energy and vitality for caring for her children when they are small. And she will have many years before becoming an Elder in which to develop her power as a woman. Also, being younger than her husband, the wife will have the energy to help care for her husband later in life — a woman never loses her mothering instincts.

There is a reason why marriages in indigenous societies tend to last a long time, and rarely end in divorce. Women are taught to always treat their husbands as twelve year-olds, because men, no matter how old they are, will throw tantrums. They pout and demand to be babied. My wife tells me I've matured with 72 winters, and now act more like a thirteen year-old.

In our society, we didn't have "teen-agers" — therefore there was no generations gap. Born free as we were, we were free to be responsible. Teenagers in indigenous society aspire to have the responsibilities and maturity of adults. The girls become adults overnight. For the boys, it takes years of maturation — years in which they are helped along their path by the women.

MARRIAGE AND CHILDREN IN THE CLAN SYSTEM

Humankind has not woven the web of life. We are but one thread within it. Whatever we do to the web, we do to ourselves. All things are bound together. All things connect... Man does not weave this web of life. He is merely a strand of it. Whatever he does to the web, he does to himself.

Seattle, Suquamish, mid 1800s

The very premise of Women is, simply, they are the Creators of Life. We built the Clan system so that we would never interfere in the communication between a Mother and her Child. We honor that communication, because of the womb. How could a woman ever be placed in a subservient role? You have a special connection to your Mother, over and above your Father or any other being. So we built this society that does not interfere with that relationship. That's why in-laws do not talk to their mothers-in-law, and vice-versa—nobody interrupts that special relationship between the Mother and Child.

The Clan System also ensures instant conflict resolution and it prevents incest at any and all levels of society. Therefore, the Husband or Wife doesn't have to feel like there is anyone intruding in the relationship between them and their Mother or within their marriage.

Regarding the husband, his Father-in-Law and Brothers-in-Law have their roles too. They constantly tease him about real or imagined foibles, accusing him of being lazy, dishonest, disloyal, and so on. So in order to make this teasing fun, and to allow him to tease back, he has to constantly strive to make sure that none of these accusations are true.

To honor their marriage, a married man or married woman are never allowed to be alone with a member of the opposite sex. If this should be found to happen by accident, both will immediately excuse themselves, to avoid any embarrassment.

If any offense is made within the Clan system, the entire family takes responsibility, immediately. If you insult someone, steal something, or inflict physical harm, then the entire family is shamed and restitution is made, both to the offended individual and to their family.

As an individual who is the Center of the Universe, you don't want to bring shame or trouble to your family. So there are no pay-backs, no revenge—this is another word and concept we do not have in indigenous languages.

Decisions within the Clan system are made by consensus only, you only do something when it is unanimous. There is no oppression by the majority.

FATHERHOOD

It is strictly believed and understood by the Lakotah that a child is the greatest gift from Wakan Tanka, in response to many devout prayers, sacrifices, and promises. Therefore the child is considered "sent by Wakan Tanka..."
                    Robert Higheagle, Teton Lakotah, early 1900s

The first duty of Fatherhood begins at conception. To begin with, it's important to understand that instead of measuring pregnancy by 3 trimesters, like the white man, we have four trimesters, or quadmesters.

Indigenous women know when they are ovulating, they know precisely when the egg is released because they are in touch with their bodies and its natural rhythms and cycles. This is how they are able to practice population control so effectively, having children at reasonable intervals, ensuring that each new child is able to grow up uncrowded by siblings, getting the proper attention they need for healthy development.

For the first 3 months — the first quadmester — the Father gets down by his Wife's stomach and sings to the developing infant. He sings lullabies and other comforting songs, letting the growing child know of his presence and his care and love. During the second 3 months, the Father sings and talks to the child in his Wife's womb. The third quadmester involves mostly talking by the Father, but also some singing.

The fourth quadmester, which commences when the

child emerges from the womb, is when the Father takes complete responsibility for caring for the newborn, except for feeding time. Every time the baby cries, it's the Father's responsibility to take the newborn and comfort and console it. The Father learns nurturing in this way, and the entire village sees this, including the young children. Everyone sees and acknowledges the Father's vital role in his family and his newborn's life.

Western science has found that it takes 3 months after childbirth for a woman to regain her physical strength and recover fully from the experience. So with the man taking on all responsibilities during this period of time, and getting a small glimpse into what it's like to be a mother, there is also the added benefit of the mother never falling prey to post-partum depression or any of the other stresses of being overwhelmed by new motherhood and all the responsibilities associated with it.

When a man has had the experience of caring for his infant in this way, a bond is forged that cannot be duplicated. The Father gets another small peek at the bond between Mother and Child. Father and Child are then enveloped within the fabric of this Mother/Child relationship, and are connected for life. Would a father with this kind of bond with his child ever advocate war, sending this child off to kill and die for some strategic purpose?

Among some indigenous people, the birth of a child is so sacred, such a miracle, that everything about childbirth remains exclusively in the province of the female, and men are allowed no participation in the process. Among the Lakotah of the High Plains, however, Fathers are more involved. Nevertheless, men respect that the miracle of creating life is primarily the province of women.

In the Christian Bible, in the Book of Genesis, you read about the story of Cain and Abel, and what happens when two children are born to the same mother too close together. Indigenous people already know that when children are born too closely together, envy will arise as the need of the children for their mother's love is severely compromised.

So what do indigenous people do in the case of twins? In the Clan system, the clan sister of the mother, or a cousin, or a blood sister who is equally close, will take and raise one of the twins as her own. The adults look to the future, thinking of what is best for the children. This way there isn't any jealousy, envy or competition among the twins, no fighting for the love of one mother.

THE CHILD IS THE CENTER OF THE UNIVERSE

It takes a village to raise a child.

West African Saying

This West African wisdom is actually a common belief among indigenous people world-wide. The First Rule of the Child in indigenous communities is, "The Child is the Center of the Universe." Every birth is celebrated as if the Supreme Being has been born. Everybody brings gifts. And from the birth onward, every child is raised as if they are the Center of the Universe.

For example, if a group of adults is discussing business, and a child should enter their sphere, all conversation of adult business stops, adult activity ceases, and all attention turns to the child. From this, the child gains feelings of self-importance, a strong personal identity, and they gain a sense of responsibility from seeing all these adults being responsible to the child. If I as a person am this significant to all these adults, then I must be an individual who matters in the grand scheme of things.

A child in this culture never hears the word "No." Both adults and older children simply give the child whatever he or she wants, thereby eliminating wishing and wanting.

By the age of 6, all cultures understand that the child is ready to leave the side of the Mother. At this age, males begin to teach the child the building blocks of discipline. Also participating in this process are older community members of both sexes, Aunties and Uncles, Grandparents...

Never deprived, the child has no material wants. He or she aspires to be gentle, firm, honorable, and responsible, in the same way they have been treated by adults and older children. A child should never cry, except as a reaction to some physical hurt, like a minor accident, common to children everywhere.

Once a child is old enough to walk, in the morning after being fed by their mother, children of 8 or 9 years will typically take the smaller children with them to play together in some section of the village. Here the small child interacts with others of all ages. An auntie might feed them a snack. The child might take a nap in the Tipi of a friend or relative, feeling safe and secure in the bosom of the community.

At this point, other children around the ages of 8 or 9 might take the child to play in another part of the village, and in this way children make the circuit of the community, knowing and becoming known by all, as in an extended family. The child learns social intercourse and social discipline, and is nurtured by people throughout the village.

By suppertime, the child comes home for the family meal. After this comes time with Grandma and Grandpa, when they take the child to visit their friends among the generation of Elders. The child gets to hear stories and create bonds of friendship among people of all generations in the community.

THE LESSON OF THE GIVEAWAY

Children were encouraged to develop strict discipline and a high regard for sharing. When a girl picked her first berries and dug her first roots, they were given away to an Elder so she would share her future success. When a child carried water for the home, an Elder would give compliments, pretending to taste meat in water carried by a boy or berries in that of a girl. The child was encouraged not to be lazy and to grow straight like a sapling.

Mourning Dove, Salish, early 1900s

It was our belief that the love of possessions is a weakness to be overcome. Its appeal is to the material part, and if allowed its way, it will in time disturb one's spiritual balance. Therefore, children must early on learn the beauty of generosity. They are taught to give what they prize most, that they may taste the happiness of giving.

Ohiyesa, Wahpeton Santee Lakotah, early 1900s

In a Lakotah village, every New Moon is marked with a feast and Giveaway. Traditionally, 8 and 9 and 10 year-olds would make gifts, and give them away to the smaller children, under 6. Nowadays, these gifts are usually toys that can be bought cheaply.

This empowers the older children, familiarizing them with the good feelings of being generous and benevolent. They become familiar with the feelings of respect that the younger children show them. This becomes a cycle of empowerment, as the younger children also see their slightly older friends and siblings enjoying the benefits of being generous and honorable. Even while enjoying being on the receiving end of the gift-giving, the younger children aspire to become 8 years old so that they can be the ones giving gifts away.

NO BAD APPLES

Among the Indians there have been no written laws.
Customs handed down from generation to generation have been the
only laws to guide them. Everyone might act different from what
was considered right if he chose, but such acts would bring upon him
the censure of the Nation... This fear of the Nation's censure acted as
a mighty bond, binding all in one social, honorable compact.

Kah-ge-ga-gah-bowh, Ojibwa, 1800s

Once a child reaches the age of 6 or 7, the men begin to include them more and more in their activities. The children are encouraged to make up their own rules to govern their play. This way, they will be sure to honor them.

Because life is so family-based, any aberration is immediately addressed, at every level—in interactions with other children clear on up to the Elders. With one bad apple capable of spoiling the barrel, you cannot afford to have any bad apples.

You are taught as a child to avoid any man you see who is alone, a loner. You rarely if ever see one in Indian society. A child that loses his temper easily is shunned by other children, and learns to control his temper that way. Other character weaknesses are addressed among the children by teasing, a great disciplinary tool in a tightly knit community.

BORN INTO A LIFE OF FREEDOM

I was born upon the prairie, where the wind blew free, and there was nothing to break the light of the sun. I was born where there were no enclosures, and where everything drew a free breath... I have hunted and lived over that country. I lived like my fathers before me, and like them, I lived happily.

Ten Bears, Comanche, late 1800s

Childhood in an indigenous society is a perfect example of living in a balanced and nurturing way of life. Anywhere in the world where indigenous people are still living the way they've always lived, in balance, and in a nurturing state, there isn't any overpopulation. We have living proof on every inhabited continent, and on islands scattered throughout the oceans. Indigenous people have lived in all kinds of environments, for generation after generation, without overpopulation.

The Hunter-Gatherer, raised in a society that puts a premium value on balance, is the epitome of human life. Modern anthropologists have observed indigenous hunter-gatherers, and found that about two hours per day is spent in fulfilling one's material responsibilities—procuring food, clothing and shelter. Compare this with the "modern" man in industrialized society, where a minimum of 8 hours per day is spent working to cover the bare essentials of life.

The Patriarch, with his industrialization, is at the bottom of the food chain. It is a complete fall from grace. The Patriarch has no connection with anything natural. Patriarchs want to conquer Natural Law, and they even admit it. Living in a Patriarchy will almost inevitably turn its subjects into a force for evil. Patriarchal religions strive to eradicate those with different beliefs. Governments force you to align with one side or the other, both of which strive to oppress the minority point of view.

THE TOXIC PATRIARCH

We are afraid that if we lose any more of our lands the white people will not leave us enough to bury our dead.
                                                    Doublehead, Creek, 1796

The so-called "development" of the human species and human societies has moved humankind not toward improving relations between peoples, or between humans and their environment, but has in fact been in the direction of destroying life—at every level, from the microscopic to the macroscopic. Instead of working within a balanced system of mutually supportive healthy life forms, human "advancement" has specialized in killing certain "undesirable" life forms, thereby opening the way for the rampant and uncontrolled proliferation of opportunistic life forms, scavengers and parasites.

Patriarchal systems everywhere are based on the idea of continued growth—specifically, growth that increases the power and wealth of the Patriarch, the few on the top of the pyramid, at the expense of the mass of people and life forms supporting them. Unending economic growth requires unending population growth, at the cost of a healthy Earth of limited resources, the cost of future generations, the cost of everything...and yet, the power of the Patriarch grows only when the human population under his dominion grows. And the only way the human population can continue to grow is via the destruction of other life. Meanwhile we have the living proof, all around the world, of indigenous people living in healthy, ecologically stable societies, since time immemorial...too happy to know better.

Any population of plants or animals that becomes excessive in number develops variants, disorders and/or diseases that act to limit or reduce their numbers. Homosexuality becomes more prevalent in any situation where animals become overcrowded, and has been observed in stressed populations of numerous mammal species in addition to humans. Like couples who delay reproduction until their 30s, or limit their families to one or two children, similar adaptations to crowded conditions appear in societies all over the world.

Unnatural living conditions have additional consequences. Europe became "plagued" with the plague only after Patriarchal systems were imposed and the entire continent became overcrowded with humans living in filthy conditions. The incidence of serial killers has increased with the growth of cities. War becomes endemic. Famine is a way of life throughout many areas of the Patriarchal world.

Humans are not row plants that thrive in a domesticated setting, we are free, wild, living in the natural world, nurturing and being nurtured by the world around us. If you want a clear demonstration of the contrast between indigenous people living matriarchally and the modern subjects of the patriarch, simply compare a wild salmon to a farm fish. Wild salmon live in deep clean water, they're fast-moving, chasing their food, surviving by being fit and healthy. Their flesh is bright-colored and firm, free of disease and parasites. Farmed salmon are pale and mushy, sickly, covered with sores, infested with worms and parasites, the victims of confinement, inactivity, unhealthy diet. Does this remind you of anyone?

THE GLOOMY REALITY OF THE PATRIARCH

Sell a country! Why not sell the air, the great sea, as well as the Earth?...How can we have confidence in the white people? When Jesus Christ came upon the Earth you killed Him and nailed Him to the cross... Where today are the Pequot? Where are the Narragansett, the Mohican, the Pocanet, and other powerful tribes of our people? They have vanished before the greed and oppression of the white man, like snow before the summer sun...the bones of our dead will be plowed up, and their graves turned into plowed fields...
Tecumseh, Shawnee, 1811

Patriarchy is imperialism—oppression and exploitation of "the other" began as soon as patriarchy reared its ugly head over 6,000 years ago. Patriarchs are masters at justifying any and every kind of monstrous misdeed—we grew up learning in school about the evil Puritans and how they extracted false confessions from suspected "witches" via the dunking stool and other tortures...and now suddenly waterboarding and other forms of torture are a good idea when applied to suspected "terrorists"—even though all evidence refutes the effectiveness of such techniques. You can say this for the Patriarch—he certainly is consistent in his irrational inconsistency.

Science is the religion of the Patriarch. This is not to be confused with Indian Science, which is based on gleaning truths from observing the natural world in action. There's nothing natural about the science that supports the monumental misdeeds and injustices of the patriarchal system. Like any religion, the Patriarch's version of "science" is replete with ritual, dogma, sacrosanct texts, articles of faith. These are all tools that are used to reinforce patriarchy. Scientists rip apart monkeys and dogs for research. How is this acceptable to anyone with the slightest shred of "humanity"? Science is utilized as a weapon by the Patriarch, in the hands of the Patriarch science becomes a killing machine. The nazis prided themselves as extremely scientific—at what cost to their humanity? Scientific research runs rampant, and yet to what end? Human lifespan is increasing incrementally but still falls short of indigenous societies—cultures famous for longevity around the world today are not in scientific societies, but are in places where people live very naturally. In scientific societies the aged are housed in inhumane warehouses, alzheimer's and dementia are increasing. Parkinsons disease never existed before the onslaught of the Industrial Revolution.

Today, protestors of scientific research are called terrorists, and grouped with those who would destroy the very fabric of society—and yet it is scientists themselves who are the only group that threatens to truly destroy Earth's balance of life. Indigenous people lived innumerable centuries without imbalance or destruction, then in only 6,000 years of patriarchy Earth has been brought to the brink of total destruction.

In patriarchy, mass murder and destruction of every kind of life is justified by the benefits to the privileged few at the very tip of the food chain. Wall Street is no different from all the tyrannies and kingdoms of history.

LIVING BY NATURAL LAW

I love a people who have always made me welcome to the best they had...who are honest without laws, who have no jails and no poor-houses...who never take the name of God in vain...who worship God without a Bible, and I believe God loves them also...who are free from religious animosities...who have never raised a hand against me, or stolen my property, where there is no law to punish either...who never fought a battle with white men except on their own ground...and oh, how I love a people who don't live for the love of money!

George Caitlin, artist, 1830s

As Hunter-Gatherers, we watch the fox and the bear. When they eat berries, they don't eat all the berries on the bush. When bears eat honey, they don't destroy the hive, they take some and move on. There is always enough left for re-generation. So we know better than to empty out a piece of land of its food. That's how you live with Natural Law.

Hunter-Gatherers never empty out their supermarket. They cause no harm to their environment whatsoever. There is no such thing as famine among hunter-gatherers because the sources of food are incredibly varied. They know where the water is. Mother Earth is their cornucopia, with all types of animals, vegetables and fruits available in every season. Hunter-gatherers know about storing food as well, both dried foods and using root cellars. They knew the plants that were good for medicine, and where to find them.

With so little time required to devote to their own

survival, hunter-gatherers had the freedom to care for themselves and for their families. They had time to bathe, to clean their teeth, to groom themselves and each other. To live by Natural Law, without conflict. There is no conflict in Natural Law. There is no evil.

If you think about it, when a child is born, where in the world is there evil? A bear or a mountain lion, killing and eating whatever they eat, is no more evil than a human who eats what humans eat. We are mindful of everything in the natural world that we use in the course of our lives. We offer thanks to the tree that we cut for use as a tipi pole. When you revere a plant, when you revere animals, it's easy to see there isn't any evil in the natural world.

Every good thought is a prayer. That is what we believe. That is why we don't have church. Life is church, the Universe is our temple. To be conscious of the well-being of the Little People—what we call insects—that's a form of prayer.

THE LIES THEY TOLD ABOUT US

In fact, there were many whites, who, after having tried [living among the Indians], expressed a preference for the free but hazardous life of savagery to the more restrained life of civilization...

Yet, while there were whites who preferred to live like Indians, there were few, if any, Indians who regarded a completely civilized form of living as superior to their own way of life. This is true even of Indian children who were educated in the schools of the white colonists and who were later permitted to return to their own people. With the opportunity of choosing between the two ways of life, they rarely cast their lot with civilization. This was because the Indian was convinced that the white man's style of life, with its lack of freedom; innumerable laws and taxes; extremes of wealth and poverty; snobbish class divisions; hypocritical customs; private ownership of land; pent-up communities; uncomfortable clothing; many diseases; slavery to money and other false standards, could not possibly bring as much real happiness as their own way of doing things...

Raymond McCoy, author, *The Massacre of Old Fort Mackinac*

Any time a discussion begins about the relative advantages of Matriarchy versus Patriarchy, or the indigenous lifestyle as compared to the post-industrial lifestyle, a number of hoary old myths are cited by the advocates of "modernity" to discredit the savage or primitive "natural man." It is worthwhile to consider these myths one by one, and to see which, if any, have the merit of logic or evidence on their side. Remember, the conquerors wrote the history books.

54

The myth of filth—since indigenous peoples live in a society where everything is organic, and returns to the elements from which it came, there is no accumulation of trash. Add to this the fact that there was no overcrowding or over-population, and we see that what in modern times is considered trash is in the indigenous society nothing but fertilizer. With no accumulations of "trash" there was no breeding ground for disease. As for personal hygiene, who's likely to be cleaner—a "savage" who purifies himself in the Inipi every few days, or a "civilized" man who bathes once a year, or less?

The myth of disease—disease was virtually unknown before the arrival of the white man, as demonstrated by the Indians' lack of resistance to European diseases which decimated Indian populations throughout the Americas. Archaeologists were astonished to find no tooth decay among any of the pre-Columbian Indian graves they robbed.

The myth of early mortality—Elders of the plains Indians tell us that before the arrival of the whites, it was common to live 150-200 years. Since their arrival, Indian lifespan has continued to shrink—now it is 43 years on the Pine Ridge Sioux Indian Reservation.

The myth of famine—Indian people lived in balance with their environment. In times of food shortage, fewer children were born. Food supplies were myriad and diverse, not dependent on a monocrop where the failure of a single plant or animal can bring disaster.

The myth of savagery—who could be more savage than the creators of the Inquisition? Europeans are famous for the myriad forms of torture they perfected on each other—victims were drawn and quartered, burned alive, tortured on the rack...the list goes on and on.

Scalping was invented by the whites—the Dutch, specifically—to collect bounties on Indian men, women and children they murdered. Originally the bounty-hunters were required to deliver heads in order to collect their reward, but the numbers of Indians killed made lugging around a huge bouquet of heads impractical. Scalping was more efficient.

The myth of ignorance—who could be more ignorant than an entire society which, while claiming a high level of sophistication, poisons its environment and creates weapons capable of destroying all life on earth? No indigenous society on earth is so ignorant as to do either.

Literacy is often held up as a standard of intellectual sophistication or advancement. Keep in mind that literate people—those who acquire a written language—become mentally lazy, they no longer have to remember. In place of the "3 R's" of U.S. education, Lakotah schooling focuses on the "3 L's"—Look, Listen, Learn. This type of education is perfectly suited to the indigenous lifestyle wherein important knowledge is derived from Natural Law. Demonstrably, indigenous people all over the world obtain the knowledge necessary for societies to thrive over the long term, with no negative impacts to their environment. In this situation, there is clearly no need for a written language. Which system is "better"? You have to ask which system works better. If the Indians of North America are so "ignorant," why did the white invaders repeatedly need the help of the Indians in order to survive? Who is really ignorant here?

The myth of human sacrifice—in order to justify murdering, enslaving and torturing Indians to death, and stealing their gold and land, it is helpful to be able to label them as pagans, heathens, and practitioners of human sacrifice. The Spanish priests and conquistadores under Cortez spent 2 years hunting down every Aztec book they could find, throughout the Aztec Empire, and burned them all. Books on advanced astronomy, mathematics, medicine, and who knows what else—all lost, forever. How convenient, then, that there was no written proof to contradict the Spanish claims of human sacrifice and other atrocities allegedly committed by the Aztecs. The Spanish could make up any lie they wanted, and with no evidence to contradict them, these lies became part of the common public perception of the Aztecs as a cruel and bloodthirsty people.

56

However, modern-day Aztecs report — and this is corroborated by recent archaeological findings — that this is not historically accurate. Once all the Aztec books were burned, there was no longer any written documentation of the early Aztec practice of open-heart surgery. This has made it easy for the uneducated Spaniards to condemn the "savages" for practicing "human sacrifice." Grave-robbing archaeologists have found plates made of gold or ivory that were used to replace and repair skull sections that were damaged by accidents or removed for complex brain surgeries. As attested to by Aztecs in Mexico today, their ancestors were proficient in the use of herbs and roots that slowed down the heart for surgical procedures — only recently have some cultural anthropologists begun to acknowledge this fact which has been known by Aztec practitioners since pre-columbian times. This evidence supports the argument that the ceremonial rituals reported by the Spanish as human sacrifice were in fact sophisticated medical procedures.

Like the nazis, patriarchs the world over and throughout history have been well-acquainted with the time-proven tactic of demonizing your enemy — the "other" — by accusing them of your own worst crimes and atrocities. In reality, it is the patriarch who continues to practice human sacrifice today, especially in places like Texas and Florida. Accompanied by religious dogma, ritual and solemnity, the condemned (and all too frequently innocent) men and women are "scientifically" put to death. As in all human sacrifice, a god of vengeance is allegedly appeased, and some benefit is supposedly accrued, such as deterrent to future crimes — while every legitimate scientific study ever conducted has shown this "deterrent factor" to be a lie.

In war also, young men and women are sent off to fight with the certain knowledge that some will die, and their sacrifice will result in some alleged benefit. Notice it is never the patriarch who marches off to risk death — only those too young and innocent and naive to know better. And wherein lies the alleged benefit? This is human sacrifice at its sickest.

THE MYTH OF WAR

Summer is the swarming season for a type of white person called 'archaeologist'... If you ever run across one of these, and they begin asking you questions, be sure to tell them nothing but lies, because otherwise they will steal your culture...

Grandma Twinklestar, Lakotah, 1900s

The myth of war — according to many white "experts," the Indian nations of North America were engaged in almost constant warfare. These were allegedly "warlike" societies, to the degree that Indian males are still identified as "warriors."

There is a saying among the Lakotah — "Old men and mothers know the folly of engaging in battle." When disagreements could not be resolved between nations, the arguments were settled in a way that was less dangerous than an American professional football game.

When the time of Treaties began, the United States government said you have to have imaginary lines around your territory. So we drew lines on a map that encompassed the area that we covered in our travels. Now several other people, smaller groups like the Mandan, the Arikara, and the Hidatsa, lived within this larger area that we frequented, and which according to the treaties was our territory. So the white man looked at this and couldn't make sense of the situation. How can one nation's territory be within the territory of another nation? When you understand that every pine needle, every stone and grain of sand, are sacred — would you exclude human beings from that sacredness? So it was easy for us share this part of the earth with each other, and to trade together.

Among the American Indians each nation's territory, or homeland, was surrounded by shared territory where you might encounter other peoples. If young men in the shared territory should act foolish, or too rash, as young men sometimes do during contests and demonstrations of bravery and athleticism, and if someone was killed or hurt, it didn't cause a war. As is common with indigenous people around the world, we had mechanisms for resolving conflict between peoples.

Our disagreements among Indian Nations were, in the words of Vine Deloria Jr., "largely settled without the spilling of blood." For example, the Six Nations settled disputes with the game of lacrosse. The Southern Indian nations had a two-stick game very similar to lacrosse. The Indians of the mid-Atlantic region had a game resembling soccer. Of course these can be violent games, but disputes are settled without much spilling of blood. The Maori of New Zealand, who tattoo their faces with intricate patterns, settle their disputes by competing to make the scariest and most horrific facial expressions — which are made even more horrific by the tattoos. The winner is the one who makes the most terrifying expression. Incidentally, the highest insult among the Maori is to moon your enemy.

Indigenous people are often amused to hear what archaeologists write about them. More often, though, what they write is outrageous. I went to a convention of the American Association of Archaeologists — a convention of grave-robbers — in order to dispute their claim that American Indians were "warlike." I asked the assembled archaeologists, "In all the pre-Columbian graves you have robbed, have you ever found a single weapon of war? If you can produce one weapon of war from any grave, I will commit suicide right here in front of you on this stage!"

Don't you think some of these arkies would've loved to see me do myself in right there on stage, or try to talk my way out of it? However, expert at robbing graves, they knew the difference between the feather/arrowhead alignment on hunting arrows for piercing vertical ribs and man-killing arrows for piercing horizontal ribs (these are commonly found in the European graves they rob). The response to my challenge from the roomful of grave robbers? Thundering silence...

THE SACREDNESS OF COLORS

Remember, if the Creator put it there, it is in the right place.
The soul would have no rainbow if the eyes had no tears.

Anonymous

All colors are sacred to the Plains Indian. We are very aware of the sacred colors. They are part of our everyday life and our ceremonial life. The color pink, for instance, within the flower of a medicinal plant on the Great Plains and in the hills — that's one of the ways of identifying medicinal plants, they have the color pink within the buds.

The color green represents all plants, leaves, pine needles, cactus, grass.

Blue — the beautiful blue sky.

The color white signifies heat, and the clouds. White represents the South, and the shimmering heat you see rising up from the Earth.

Black is the thunderclouds, and the night. Black also represents the West.

Red represents the North, and the North Wind, which stirs the blood.

Yellow represents the Morning Star and the dawn of a new day, as well as the Sun. Yellow means you can begin a new day by not repeating the mistakes of yesterday.

Black, red, yellow and white also represent the 4 races of people, and when you mix those four colors together you get brown, the color of the other race, and the color of our Grandmother the Earth.

Purple represents the rainbow and the rain which cleanses and purifies our Grandmother Earth. It is a thanking sign.

Then you have the different hues of color at dawn and dusk, and they all have meaning—what kind of day it's going to be, what kind of day it was, and what kind of day tomorrow will be.

The Moon controls water and the color that signifies water is orange, because when the full moon rises as the sun sets, its color is orange.

By understanding the stars, we knew where the grass would grow, and where the buffalo would be to graze on it. So we didn't have to follow the dung to find the buffalo, we knew their migration routes by understanding the Stars. By Natural Law, we understood that the Moon and the Stars were involved with controlling water.

THE SAFETY NET OF THE CLAN

Before our white brothers arrived to make us civilized men, we didn't have any kind of prison. Because of this, we had no delinquents. Without a prison, there can be no delinquents. We had no locks nor keys and therefore among us there were no thieves. When someone was so poor that he couldn't afford a horse, a tent or a blanket, he would, in that case, receive it all as a gift. We were too uncivilized to give great importance to private property. We didn't know any kind of money and consequently, the value of a human being was not determined by his wealth. We had no written laws laid down, no lawyers, no politicians, therefore we were not able to cheat and swindle one another. We were really in bad shape before the white men arrived and I don't know how to explain how we were able to manage without these fundamental things that (so they tell us) are so necessary for a civilized society.

John Fire Lame Deer, Lakotah, 1900s

A Matriarchy is a nurturing, family-based society. At every level of this female-based society, a woman is in rhythm — with the Universe, with the Earth, with her family and clan.

Among the Lakotah, only a woman can get a divorce. If a woman throws a man out, it means one of two things — he is either a lousy provider, and/or a lousy lover. So if you see a man alone, no woman is going to take a chance on him. The man is shamed, he lives by himself and has no friends. With this kind of rule in place, there is essentially no divorce. There is pressure on a man to perform and he strives to learn what he is lacking in order to keep his woman happy.

Nobody acts alone in this kind of society, young men are taught what they need to know. With all his relatives helping, it is impossible for a man to be a bad provider. So if you look at the complex social structure of the indigenous Clan system, you see that divorce was impossible. It made it impossible for one to be a loser, or an outcast, because the individual was supported by his clan.

LEADERS AMONG THE LAKOTAH

Among us we have no prisons, we have no pompous parade
of courts; we have no written laws, and yet judges are as highly
revered among us as they are among you, and their decisions are as
highly regarded.

Property, to say the least, is well-guarded, and crimes are as
impartially punished. We have among us no splendid villains above
the control of our laws. Daring wickedness is never suffered to
triumph over helpless innocence. The estates of widows and orphans
are never devoured by enterprising sharpers. In a word, we have no
robbery under color of the law.

Joseph Brant, Mohawk, 1807

The woman knows that the province of the home is her domain. Because men have a more linear and practical way of thinking, their responsibilities lay outside the home—the village, the Nation.

In indigenous societies, to be a leader meant that, materially, you were always going to be poor. This is because you had to make sure everyone else in the community was taken care of. So being a leader was avoided by many men. Leaders had to be chosen, designated, by the Elder Women. So a leader among the men did not rise to the position out of personal ambition, greed for power, or personal insecurities, trying to prove something. These are all characteristics of unfit leaders, which are common among the patriarchs.

Men are chosen to be leaders in indigenous societies because of a man's unique characteristics and attributes that qualify him to be a great leader. Whether he likes it or not. And, as part of a tightly knit community, this mantle of leadership is not a burden that is borne alone by the man who is chosen as a leader. The entire village, knowing he is a leader of the people, makes sure his family is taken care of. That's one of the advantages about a society where a child grows up as the Center of the Universe—there are no wants, no envy. Mutual sharing is the norm.

In a tightly knit indigenous community, it is the family that would first take responsibility for helping those who are helpless—the widowed, crippled, aged. If it turned out that the assistance that was needed exceeded the resources of the family, then the clan, or tiospaye, would step in. If still more help was required, then the leadership would step in. The point is, everyone was well taken care of.

Being part of a caring civilization meant the members were inclined to be peace-loving. That's why we could never think of war. When you care about and are mindful of a pine needle or a blade of grass or a cloud, how could you not care about other humans and how they feel?

A good example of our mindfulness would be our horses—it took us 7 or 8 years to train a horse. We trained our horses through trust. There was no such thing as "breaking" a horse. Your horse acted around you more like a dog—you could call it and it would come, it wouldn't leave your side. And it wasn't just one horse, these relationships were developed with a plethora of horses. You were present at every birth, so that the first scent in the newborn's nostrils is you, not its mother—this way it will remember you and feel a bond with you for the rest of its life. When you're truly free you have time to develop this kind of relationship with your horses, you have time for everything, time to clean and groom your hair, time to clean your teeth, raise your children, love your family. All life was sacred.

You don't need a bit or even reins to ride a horse trained the Lakotah way. You tell your horse where you're going with your knees. Back in the days when we were free, I

—

66

was told a rider had just a loose rope around the horse's neck to hold on to. If you held their mane you'd pull out the hair, so you guided the horse by your knees and by this simple loop of rope.

PEACEMAKER

Lose your temper and you lose a friend; lie and you lose yourself.

Hopi

Peace and happiness are available in every moment. Peace is in every step. Let us walk hand in hand. There are no political solutions to spiritual problems.

Anonymous

Every village had a Peacemaker. If there were two families with irreconcilable differences, the Peacemaker would take them to a Tipi or other structure, and drape a hide or blanket across the middle so neither side could see the other. One side would explain their position in the argument, and the other side had to listen without interrupting. Then the other side would tell their story. Then each side would be asked for their recommendation for settling the dispute. This discussion would continue until there was consensus, or agreement. Nobody was ever forced into anything. Freedom was tantamount, because what good is agreement, really, if it requires coercion, and isn't arrived at freely?

If there ever was a time when consensus could not be reached, both sides knew there was an alternative solution — the minority who disagreed could, with no hard feelings, separate from the larger group and become a sister clan. These two sister clans, when meeting later, treat one another like long-lost relatives. The connection between them is more important than whatever dispute caused them to separate.

TO LIVE IN MINDFUL REVERENCE

*When a man does a piece of work which is admired by all we
say that it is wonderful...but when we see the changes of day and
night, the sun, the moon, and the stars in the sky, and the changing
seasons upon the earth, with their ripening fruits, anyone must
realize that it is the work of someone more powerful than man.*
Chased-by-Bears, Santee-Yankton Lakotah, early 1900s

A Lakotah tries to be the best person they can be for that day.
We live our entire lives under the constant, watchful, loving
eye of our Ancestors.

A man is given four different names throughout his
lifetime and he is expected to live up to these names. A
woman is given three names — first as a girl, then when she
becomes a woman, and her third name came with Elder
status, the highest and most exalted status in Lakotah
society.

The man's four names come with childhood, young
manhood, mature manhood, and upon becoming an Elder.
The names were not given at specific years or exact "times" —
remember, we were free of the neurotic belief in time. The
names were given by the Elders, the names were honorable,
and they were a constant reminder to be the best person that
one can be at all times, to live in the continual experience of
reverence.

The traditional Lakotah story of Looks Twice is a good
example of how a young man is expected to live up to his
name. Early in the spring, when the village was getting low on
food, Looks Twice went out hunting. He didn't come across

any game near the village, so he searched farther, crossing many streams and dry canyons. As he traveled, the spring weather got warmer.

Finally, miles from the village, Looks Twice came across some buffalo. Only after killing one of the buffalo did Looks Twice stop and look around, taking his bearings. To his dismay, he now noticed that the warm weather had melted snow up in the mountains, causing all the streams to rise and all the dry canyons to fill with water. Looks Twice found himself all alone, with a ton of buffalo meat, miles from the village and cut off by the rising water.

The story of Looks Twice was told to me by my grandfather, walking along the banks of the Missouri River, when I was a boy of four or five. Like all traditional Lakotah stories, this one seems to end in the middle. The child's natural response—"What happened next?!"—is met with a shrug. What do you think happened next? Traditional Lakotah stories are designed to make you think, to figure things out for yourself. Did Looks Twice live up to the name he was given? Will you do a better job than Looks Twice in living up to yours?

THE TRUE LAKOTAH STYLE BUFFALO HUNT

It would be wise to invite all the sportsmen of England and America...for a grand buffalo hunt, and make one grand sweep of them all.

General William Tecumseh Sherman, 1870s

It's important to dispel the myths regarding our buffalo hunts, and to describe the way in which we truly hunted buffalo in traditional times. There was no waste and much less drama than in the pop-culture version that has insinuated itself into the mass consciousness.

Paintings by Remington and others show a dramatic TV-style "artist's rendition" buffalo hunt, where "wild Indians" on horseback gallop recklessly alongside a furious, foaming 1-ton buffalo, firing arrows into the side of the enraged beast. This is totally unrealistic. Pursuit of a buffalo in this fashion would put ourselves and our horses at serious risk of death or injury. Remember, we spend 8 years training our horses. To put this in terms a white man can relate to, this would be like racing our brand-new BMW across the plains, over rocks and hill and dale and possibly right over a cliff. Only to our way of thinking, the horse is even more precious to us than a new BMW — the horse is also our best friend. So we would never expose our horses or ourselves to this insane risk.

In reality, we learned about how to hunt buffalo by watching the coyotes hunt buffalo. The coyotes of the northern plains are even smaller than the desert variety, they are diminutive creatures not much larger than a fox. How could animals of this small stature bring down a buffalo weighing a ton?

Coyotes chase the buffalo around in a circle until it is exhausted and easy to kill. So we do the same. In this way, by the time the buffalo is killed it is exhausted, and its blood is pumped through all the muscles. This makes it much easier to skin and butcher. The meat is moist and naturally tenderized. And we learned all this by Natural Law, by watching the coyote.

There are a number of other reasons for hunting buffalo in the coyote style. Paintings by white visitors such as Remington show a gruesome and dramatic aftermath of the hunt, where the plains are littered by numerous buffalo being skinned and butchered.

This image is a patent lie. A ton of meat — one buffalo — can feed many people. We had no refrigeration. All that meat had to be dried in order to be preserved. We killed one buffalo at a time. That's all we needed. If we killed more than one, someone would have to haul an extra ton of dried meat around until we needed it. Why not let the buffalo haul himself around until the next time we got hungry?

And we never chased buffalo for miles across the plains — who is going to go all the way out there and haul back all that meat, in addition to the hide and skull and bones? Remember, we used all parts of the buffalo, none was left to go to waste. We didn't chase an entire herd of buffalo off a cliff to be slaughtered en masse, the way Remington and the others painted it in their falsely dramatized visions of carnage and waste. No, this was the way the white buffalo hunters did it in later years, when they nearly killed every last buffalo, and when all they bothered to harvest was the tongue, leaving a ton of meat to rot with each unused carcass.

In 60 years' time, the white man exterminated 60 million buffalo, according to anthropological research. This works out to more than 83,000 per month, or about 116 an hour, or around 2 buffalo killed per minute. Wealthy Easterners paid for "Hunting Tours" by train where they chugged slowly through vast buffalo herds — the buffalo presenting easy targets as they feared neither trains nor loud noises like gunfire — shooting as many buffalo as they possibly could, and not bothering to harvest a single part of the buffalo.

We "primitive" Indians simply cut a single buffalo from the herd, chased him in a circle coyote-style until he was easily killed, and did so near the village for convenience sake.

"Primitive" is a description an indigenous person can wear with pride. The word primitive is derived from the Latin root primus, meaning first. Call any traditional Indian a "Born-Again Primitive"...and chances are you will be thanked for the compliment.

THE POWER OF EAGLES

The life of an Indian is like the winged creatures of the air.
You notice the hawk knows how to get his prey – the Indian is like
that. The hawk swoops down on its prey; so does the Indian... The
eagle is the same. That is why the Indian is always feathered up – he
is a relative to the winged ones of the air.
Black Elk, Oglala Lakotah, early 1900s

There is a reason for the strong alliance between birds and the Lakotah people, and it goes way back to the early days when it had not yet been determined which type of creature would rule here on Earth.

The four-leggeds, being bigger and stronger and more numerous than the two-leggeds, felt they should be in charge. The insect-people, being more numerous than anyone else, believed they should naturally dominate. We two-leggeds did not agree, and to settle the dispute it was agreed that a race around the Black Hills would be held, and the winner of the race would take over from that point on.

So the race began, and of course the four-leggeds charged out ahead, easily taking the lead. From up in the sky above, the birds watched the race with great interest. How could anyone among the two-leggeds or the insect-people possibly overcome the huge lead of the four-leggeds? The outcome seemed certain.

Then the birds suddenly realized that they are two-leggeds too, and that victory by the four-leggeds would not work out so well for them. So the birds joined in the race, and of course they overtook and passed the four-leggeds, winning easily. This is the reason for the dominance of the two-leggeds to this day, and the close ties between the birds and ourselves.

To this day, no Lakotah will eat a wild bird, or its eggs. We feather up in honor of the birds. Since male plumage among the birds is much more colorful than the females, the men of the Lakotah Nation honor the birds by adorning themselves with colorful beads, quill work and feathers. In photos taken by satellites, the race track around the Black Hills is still clearly visible.

The Dakota, along with the smaller nations of Mandan, Hidatsa and Ree, lived along the rivers. Before the dams were built clogging the Upper Missouri and its tributaries, these rivers were thick with sturgeon and pike and many other species of fish. These fish were the food staple of the indigenous people living there. We did not eat bottom feeders, like catfish.

Every spring when the rivers were thick with spawning fish, the eagles were attracted to feed. So these nations living along the water had a wealth of eagle feathers and fresh and dried fish, and all the jewelry that was associated with the river. This meant they had a wealth of trade goods that were unavailable to the rest of us. We would come and trade with them to supplement our diet, and to acquire eagle feathers from live eagles. Eagle feathers that come from a live eagle have Power. You can only take two feathers from any single live eagle, one from each wing or one from each side of the tail feathers.

This required a particular type of ceremony. We had our own ceremony called the "Calling of Eagles" ceremony, where we captured a live eagle, took two feathers and then set the eagle free. We only wore eagle feathers around our heads, near our brains, and these were exclusively from live eagles.

Nowadays, eagle feathers generally come from dead eagles, killed in the many nefarious ways of modern industrial society, and these feathers from dead eagles are worn around the butt. It has always been dishonorable to kill an eagle for any reason. If you see an Indian at a modern-day Indian dance, or pow-wow, with an eagle feather, you know that eagle was killed. Those are dead eagle feathers. This is an aberration that never happened until the 1950s. To the purist who knows our ways, it is a public dishonor to wear those eagle feathers around the butt, or to have an entire eagle wing as part of a dance or ceremonial outfit.

This is yet another example of how the Heyoka has permeated our culture, and how the Heyoka way is alive and well, and thriving. The aberration of wearing dead eagle feathers was able to take place when it did only because of the disbanding of the Honorable Shirt Wearers Society.

THE HONORABLE SHIRT WEARERS SOCIETY
OF THE LAKOTAH NATION

I did not know then how much was ended. When I look back now from this high hill of my old age, I can still see the butchered women and children lying heaped and scattered all along the crooked gulch as plain as when I saw them with eyes still young. And I can see that something else died there in the bloody mud, and was buried in the blizzard. A people's dream died there. It was a beautiful dream...the nation's hoop is broken and scattered. There is no center any longer, and the sacred tree is dead.

Black Elk, Oglala Lakotah, early 1900s

Prior to World War II, Indians across the United States had been successfully confined to the federal reservation system of America. Then World War II allowed thousands of young Indian men to enter the armed services. Upon the survivors' return from the war, the Elders witnessed how much the young men had been changed from their experience in the patriarchal white world.

The Honorable Shirt Wearers Society of my nation were charged with maintaining our life ways and cultural values. All nations had similar societies. The Shirt Wearers Society saw how the hearts and minds of the young men were changed, and the Elders saw that our traditional way of life was over. In 1946 and 1947, the Shirt Wearers Society took off their shirts and buried them.

A COMMON LANGUAGE

Behold, my brothers, the spring has come. The Earth has received the embraces of the sun and we shall soon see the results of that love. Every seed has awakened and so has all animal life. It is through this mysterious power that we too have our being, and we therefore yield to our neighbors, including our animal neighbors, the same right as ourselves — to inhabit this land.
Tatanka Yotanka (Sitting Bull), Hunkpapa Lakotah, late 1800s

All the Plains Indians and all those who lived on the edge of America's central plains, stretching from central Canada to north central Mexico, shared a thorough system of communication, based on sign language. It takes a long time to learn sign language. This was a universal language that stretched from the Lower Missouri, Texas and Oklahoma and northern Mexico where the Comanche and Kiowa lived, all the way north into the plains of Canada, the Blackfoot Confederacy of Alberta, Saskatchewan and parts of Manitoba, and west throughout the Rocky Mountain region, including the vast Shoshone Nation which extended across Nevada and Southern California clear to the Pacific Ocean.

Anthropologists have studiously ignored the fact that all these societies shared a universal language. The people that you share language with are your relatives. We had relatives all the way down past Oklahoma and Texas into Mexico. We were speaking and communicating and trading with one another, not waging war. If you take the time to communicate, you're not going to have war. It's when you don't take the time to communicate that you wage war.

As we mentioned before, there is no such thing as war in indigenous societies, just as there is no such thing as evil. This fact is so important and so overlooked that it is worth repeating. There was no experience of anything resembling the warfare that became a common feature within and among patriarchal cultures. It was not in our language, and if it's not in the language, you don't have the concept. It simply doesn't exist—how can a society follow a practice they've never heard of?

CURSED WITH THE POWER OF REASON

We ought to name this place in honor of the Yellow Thunder family, because after Raymond Yellow Thunder was murdered in Gordon South Dakota, the Lakotah stood up as a people for the first time in this century.

Russell Means, 1981

In 1981, about 50 Indians and like-minded whites reclaimed the Black Hills, which by International Treaty legally belong to the Lakotah people, by establishing a traditional settlement there called Yellow Thunder Camp. Camping was legal in the Black Hills, so I was able to live there without breaking parole from an earlier conviction following a "police riot" and courthouse burning in Custer, South Dakota. While serving that prison sentence I was stabbed in the chest with an ice pick by a white supremacist who was released soon after for "good behavior." In those days Indians in South Dakota were commonly referred to as "prairie niggers," and stores displayed large signs reading "No Dogs, No Indians."

Yellow Thunder Camp, in the Lakotah Holy Land, provided an opportunity to learn much about traditional life and Natural Law. One day I threw a rock into Victoria Lake, about the size of a beaver pond, and as the series of concentric waves spread outward from the point of impact I had a profound realization — if you envision that central point as your heart, then the nearest circle can be seen as your family. The next circle would be your extended family, followed by your clan, your nation, the world, the Universe...into Infinity.

In this way I saw that my heart is connected to and affects Infinity...with this connection in mind—knowing that your heart has an effect on the Infinite—you see how important it is to have a pure and healthy heart! Our hearts are part of the Infinite, not separate from it.

American Indians see all life as a combination of sacrifice, suffering, sharing, gifts and teachings. When we go out to get a pole for our Tipi, we give thanks to the tree for its sacrifice.

We learn, from the force of the river or creek during high water in the spring flood, that you don't allow water to divide you, because water is a powerful force, and if it wants to destroy you, it will.

We two-leggeds are not at the top of the food chain, we're at the bottom, because of all the creatures on Earth we're the only ones who are cursed with the power of reason. We don't know the things we need to know to function in life by instinct, the way all other animals do. This is why we have to learn from all our relatives—all the children of the Earth Mother are our teachers.

RISE OF THE HEYOKA

Here I stand, and the tree is withered. Again, I recall the great vision you gave me. It may be that some little root of the sacred tree still lives. Nourish it then, that it may leaf and bloom and fill with singing birds! Hear me, that the people may once again find the good road and the shielding tree.

Black Elk, Oglala Lakotah, early 1900s

Homosexuals and the transgendered were held in high esteem in our society. They became teachers because of their different world view, and our children can benefit from this — we want them to be exposed to, and to learn from, all different world views.

People who were handicapped were teachers as well. They weren't seen as outsiders, outcasts, or as different from anyone else in essence, in spirit. We understood that we could learn a great deal from those whose unique circumstances caused them to adapt in individual ways. Cripples strengthened the fabric of our society.

Living among us we also had the Heyoka, people who live backwards, as a constant reminder that you can't live backwards in this world. Heyoka have to enter their Tipi backwards, they have to go to sleep at dawn and get up at dusk. By giving you a constant reminder of how hard it is to live this way, they help us to keep our lives on a straighter path.

Heyokas were rare when we were free. But we knew about them, and if there were none in our particular village, we were told about them. The basic premise of a Heyoka is as a teacher, teaching us how not to live by doing everything backwards in the physical sense. Walking backwards, talking backwards — so he's always talking about bad things, but it means the opposite. So he is a teacher. And the further you get away from the Great Mystery's teachings, the more Heyokas are needed.

In Pine Ridge back in the 1960s, there was only one Heyoka in the entire nation. That is because most of the old people who kept our culture alive were still living. But as they died off, more Heyokas materialized. Now practically every Holy Man is Heyoka. This means the people aren't listening to the teaching. The whole nation is becoming Heyoka. With so many people becoming addicted to one drug or another, and sending their kids to school where they learn the antiknowledge of the Patriarch, the whole nation is unwittingly turning Heyoka—they don't even realize it. There may be only a few left in the Lakotah Nation who are Medicine Men working in the tradition of the Ordinary Man, that is, not Heyoka.

A Heyoka is not 100% backwards. When they do things as a Heyoka—that is, backwards—they should be acutely aware of what they are doing, as a Medicine Man working in the Heyoka tradition. Only a few great ones know that they are Heyoka these days. The others are Heyoka, teaching backwards, without even knowing it. This has become the tragic norm.

THE INVERTED REALITY OF THE HEYOKA
AND THE PATRIARCH

To take and to lie should be burned on his forehead, as he burns the sides of my stolen horses with his own name.

Charlot, Flathead, 1876

The entire system and world view of the patriarch is Heyoka. Patriarchy is based on a pyramid structure. The Patriarch is uncomfortable everywhere he goes. He is afraid because he lives his life teetering at the top of the pyramid, and others are constantly trying to push him off his perch. Within his family, his wife and children must be enslaved in order to support his position of prominence and dominance. His children are brought up in his own image, to be fearful patriarchs tottering at the peak of their own unstable pyramid.

If he wants to maintain this position among his family, the Patriarch must be subjugated to the next level of authority, and so on up to royalty. Feudal structure, where nobody is free and the man on top is afraid of everything, is the natural product of patriarchy. Everybody within the patriarchal system is a slave, because every person below the ultimate ruler is a slave to the power of all the patriarchs above them. And even the man at the very pinnacle of the pyramid is a slave — a slave to his own terror, of being toppled from power.

In our Matriarchal system, everyone is free and nobody is afraid of anything. We know who we are and where we belong. This can never be taken away from us. This is why the patriarchs have struggled so long and hard to destroy us and our cultures the world over. We are a terrible threat to his illusion of power because we are immune to it. He can commit complete genocide and wipe out entire indigenous cultures again and again, but he has never succeeded in enslaving us. Our freedom from fear makes the Patriarch more fearful than ever.

IKTOMI — THE TRICKSTER

He has filled graves with our bones...his course is destruction, he spoils what the spirit who gave us this country made beautiful and clean...the white man fathers this doom...he, the cause of our ruin, is his own snake which he says stole on his mother in her own country to lie to her. He says his story is that man was rejected and cast off... He says one of his virgins had a son nailed to death on two cross sticks to save him. Were all of them dead when that young man died, we would all be safe now, and our country would still be our own.

Charlot, Flathead, 1876

In our mythology that we teach our children we have the Legend of the Two-Faced. Nobody, not even the white man, can lead a two-faced life. However the Iktomi can be two-faced, in fact he's always two-faced.

The white man is always confused by the concept of Iktomi, who is often represented by the Spider. American Indian people don't believe in the Devil. We don't believe in evil. We had no experience of it, until we met a patriarch.

A basic premise among indigenous people is that there isn't anything that is perfect. So you build this idea into the society, and therefore you have Iktomi, the Trickster. Iktomi is a teacher, he will teach you about the tricks of life, the foibles of life, about temptation, about egos.

In the first 5 years of life, you are given a thorough introduction to the Iktomi. The stories you hear as a small child school you in the imperfections of life, through the tales of the Iktomi, the Trickster. There is nothing evil about him. Iktomi, by the way, is a male.

Think about all the phenomena that occur naturally in the world—a baby, a bear, a bee, a spider, the wind, a snowstorm...what is evil? Thinking logically, how can this label be attached to anything we might encounter in the natural world? There isn't anything evil in the world, everything is as it should be, nothing can be evil. In fact we give thanks for the snowstorm that covers our Grandmother Earth with a blanket of snow in a time of cold. So Iktomi, as part of the natural world, is not evil, in fact he can be downright funny. But you've got to look out. That's the lesson of Iktomi.

THE EARTH IS A LIVING CREATURE

How can you buy or sell the sky, the warmth of the land? The idea is strange to us. If we do not own the freshness of the air and sparkle of the water, how can you buy them?... This beautiful Earth is the mother of the red man. We are part of the Earth and it is part of us.

Seattle, Suquamish, mid 1800s

A team of scientists sank a shaft into our Grandmother Earth, in Greenland, they sank it miles deep and brought up data for a few years. Their conclusion was that she—the Earth—is a living being! This data, this knowledge, leads naturally to an astounding and disturbing question—if the Earth is alive, why aren't these same scientists more concerned about killing her? About raping her? About the relentless damage and destruction caused by "extractive" industries such as mining, logging, and drilling for oil?

Maybe it's not so shocking that male scientists are not overly concerned about killing the Earth. After all, the Earth is a "she," and in a patriarchal society not much value is placed on anything female or feminine. But it is an astonishing aspect of the Feminist Movement, that in their desperate craving to be just like men, feminists who want to become powerful figures in the socio-economic system eagerly lead the charge in killing and raping the ultimate female, Grandmother Earth.

Look at the Olympic Games, do you see any contests about etiquette, or any feminine activities of any kind? All the women's events are just men's events with women competing against each other to be better men. Where is the Olympic Games of nurturing? On how to develop a sixth sense, Intuition? Where is the Olympics on the miracle of creating life? Why is the Feminist Movement so anti-Feminine?

THERE IS NO FEAR OF DEATH IN THE INDIGENOUS WORLD

There is no death...only a change of worlds.
Seattle, Suquamish, mid 1800s

It quickly becomes clear that the indigenous person does not fear "death." We know our place in the Universe. Every spring we see reincarnation in action. Leaves sprout anew, flowers bloom again.

Indigenous societies are the epitome of being free. We live free of fear, anxiety, angst. Everything is taken care of for us, provided for us plentifully by Grandmother Earth.

When you are free, and you have time for everything, and you are never in a hurry. This is true freedom. Time is a human construct, it is not part of the natural world. The way we look at time is that there is no such thing as time, therefore time cannot control or limit you or work against you. If anything, time is on your side. Time is not some external reality that you must conform to. There are no dictates in time. You can choose to acknowledge it or not.

Archeologists have robbed more than enough graves of our ancestors to ascertain that there wasn't any disease among our people, we didn't even have tooth decay. Our ancestors developed and produced seventy-five percent of the world's food being used today. We were so advanced in the medicinal use of plants that pharmaceutical companies are still sending their minions into the jungles of Ecuador and Brazil, searching for ever-more medicinal herbs and plant-based drugs used in indigenous medical practices that the multinationals can then exploit for billions of dollars in profit.

We indigenous people had time to notice the world around us, and to learn from it, and that is why we develop all these practices and all this knowledge which is still so elusive to the patriarch. Foremost among these gifts is the ability to be happy, to be satisfied. There are no neurotics among us.

THE BALANCE AND HOLINESS OF ALL THINGS

The Earth is the Mother of all people, and all people should
have equal rights upon it...
Chief Joseph, Nez Perce, late 1800s

It's funny that the Human Being is physically constructed like Grandmother Earth—2/3 water. Both Earth and the human body host vast colonies of diverse Life. Earth, through her own functions, continuously purifies herself. When humans remain cognizant of Earth's natural processes of purification, the humans do the same—they strive to continuously purify themselves through natural processes, maintaining balance. All of life must be in balance.

Indigenous people the world over who have always lived by the cycles of Earth and the Universe are now getting out of balance because these cycles have been disrupted. Balance—what does this mean? Living in balance comes from an understanding of Natural Law.

One learns Natural Law from observing all the different forms of life around us—plant life, four-leggeds of every kind, the insect people, the winged people...humans are subject to the same laws or principles as everything else in the Universe.

Once any life form starts to overpopulate, the Great Mystery, or whatever force it is that governs all things, will begin to create natural mechanisms that begin to limit population growth and bring things back into balance. For example, among mammals, when overpopulation threatens the balance, lemmings hurl themselves into the sea and commit suicide en masse. This happens among humans as well—though it takes many different forms. Drug abuse, alcoholism, violent crime, warfare. This is Natural Law at work.

Health and balance are closely interwoven. If a society creates an accumulation of garbage, a breeding ground for disease now exists. However if a people live in balance, according to Natural Law, no accumulation of garbage ever exists. The by-products of American Indian life have always been completely natural materials, not toxic either to humans or any other co-residents of Earth. Even human bodily waste, when not accumulated in large quantities from excessive populations, is not toxic. In fact it's the opposite, decomposing into the elements and in the process providing raw materials and nourishment for more life. Everything used by American Indians living by Natural Law will revert back to the building blocks of new life.

Recently you have probably heard the patriarchs talking about "carbon credits" – the basis for "value" in today's scientific system is each individual's right to contribute their share of pollution—that is, to do their pro-rata share of murdering the Earth and her natural systems that we all depend on to survive. They're even talking about how the individual may in the near future be able to sell their carbon credits to some polluting industry. There may come into existence a "stock exchange" upon which carbon credits are bought, sold and traded. Just by being born, the patriarch entitles himself to participate equally in the destruction of Earth. This is a sad self-image. The basis for currency, for things of value, used to be precious metals—now value is based on filth and universal genocide, including "maso-genocide"—genocide toward oneself.

If a people lives by and obeys Natural Law, there is no need for man-made laws for any situation. The very first man-made law is the death of Natural Law. Once a man-made law is created, man has become God, the maker of laws, and the entire purpose of human existence has been defeated.

Natural Law is the law of life, man-made law is the law of death. This applies to the family unit as well. Once man-made law is imposed on the family unit, normal patterns of nurturing are disrupted. Each nuclear family becomes its own autocratic domain, where freedom by the young is achieved only through leaving the family unit and starting their own dictatorial family unit. Under Natural Law, the extensive interwoven family structure remains growing stronger and more interconnected as new generations come into being.

We don't build churches, and go inside to pray one day per week. We pray outside, in the Natural World. And our entire life is an act of prayer, because there is Holiness in all things in the Natural World here on Grandmother Earth.

THE UNIVERSE

*You have noticed that everything an Indian does is in a
circle, and that is because the power of the world always works in
circles, everything tries to be round... The sky is round, and I have
heard that the Earth is round like a ball, and so are all the stars. The
wind, in its greatest power, whirls. Birds make their nests in circles,
for theirs is the same religion as ours... Even the seasons form a great
circle in their changing, and always come back again to where they
were. The life of a man is a circle from childhood to childhood, and so
it is in everything where power moves.*

Black Elk, Oglala Lakotah, early 1900s

The Universe is our tabernacle, it's our house of worship. To
understand this house, we must understand the Stars. All life
is connected, the Stars including the Sun are connected with
the Planets and the Moon. The Stars also give us direction.
When we pay attention to what's going on in the sky
overhead, the Universe tells us and shows us the answers to
the mysteries of life.

By observation, we see that all things travel in a circle.
The circling Stars show us that the Universe moves in a circle.
The Earth circles the Sun. The Moon moves in a circle, as does
Earth herself. Seasons of the year and other natural rhythms
come in cycles—summer to winter, sunrise to sunset, the
Moon rises and sets as it also cycles from Full Moon to New
Moon. The Moon, circling through her cycles, controls the
cycles of water here on Earth. The Moon also controls the
purification cycle of Woman.

Just like any creation story, we have stories of coming from the Stars to the water, and then being born out of water from the Woman—who is purified naturally, through water.

The Sun is male, Earth is female. Earth goes through cycles of birth, dormancy and purification through water, and Woman follows the same pattern. The Sun gives energy to the Earth so that life can be created out of her, just as Man gives his seed to Woman.

All life began in Water. Water is sacred, never to be despoiled. Earth and Woman are the most sacred of beings, they are Holy, because they create life from the energy of the Sun/Man.

Because Woman is more Holy than Man, she lives longer, she can withstand more pain, she has more endurance, and she has a unique 6th sense that cannot be explained.

Woman goes through two changes in life—from a girl, she blossoms into womanhood, and after her childbearing years she transitions into an Elder. Man, just like the Sun, goes through no changes—from the time he reaches manhood, he just goes and goes until burnout. He is never naturally purified, Man is 1-dimensional compared to Woman. However, like the Woman, he does travel through life in a circle—from diaper to diaper. The tides, that rise and fall under control of the Moon, and that are endlessly cyclical, are representative of all life on Earth.

EPILOGUE

There is a road in the hearts of all of us, hidden and seldom traveled, which leads to an unknown, secret place. The old people came literally to love the soil, and they sat or reclined on the ground with a feeling of being close to a mothering power. Their tipis were built upon the Earth and their altars were made of earth. The soil was soothing, strengthening, cleansing and healing. That is why the old Indian still sits upon the Earth instead of propping himself up and away from its life-giving forces. For him, to sit or lie upon the ground is to be able to think more deeply and to feel more keenly. He can see more clearly into the mysteries of life and come closer in kinship to other lives around him.

Luther Standing Bear, Oglala Lakotah, early 1900s

In the 1960s, an elder Déné man from the Northwest Territories of Canada stated to an anthropologist who was intent on civilizing the Déné people, "You white people are very arrogant. You think you are responsible for the extinction of different forms of life. Have you ever considered that maybe those life forms didn't want to live with you?"

The Kogi Indians of South America live high on an 18,000-foot mountain on the edge of the Caribbean Sea. They have preserved their culture intact since before the arrival of the Conquistadores in the lowlands below their mountain. Their society is run by priests, called *Mamas*, who are trained from birth to assume the spiritual and political leadership of a people who call themselves the "Big Brothers." All Patriarchal societies of the world are referred to by the Kogi "Little

Brothers."

The Kogi believe that the Earth is a living being, and that the mountain on which they live is a bellwether of the health of the Earth. It is the duty of the Kogi Mamas, through deep meditation and the preservation of certain sacred sites, to keep the Earth in balance and maintain her health.

For centuries before the invasion of the Spanish, and for all the centuries since, the Kogi have managed to maintain the health and vigor of the Earth on which we all depend for survival. Lately, however, things have begun to change for the worse. Species have died off or disappeared from their mountain home. The water cycle is disrupted., and avocado trees and other plants have withered and died. Avalanches have wreaked carnage. The mountain is dying. And with it, the Earth.

Recently the Kogi, who have long been reclusive and avoided contact with the Little Brothers, have descended from the mountain to spread the warning to all people. They have even established a website to make sure that their message is heard loud and clear by all people around the world.

The activities of the Little Brothers have become too destructive. The Kogi can no longer keep the Earth healthy on their own. The Earth is dying and to save it, the Big Brothers need the help of the Little Brothers.

It is still not too late. The living Earth can be saved — and with her, the lives of all of us who depend on her. But the Little Brothers will have to change their way of living on the Earth. Otherwise, say the Kogi, their holy mountain will die, and the Little Brothers will bring upon us all the end of all life on Earth.

In the words of Chief Seattle, "Nation follows nation like the waves of the sea, it is the order of Nature, and regret is useless. Your time of decay may be distant, but it will surely come, for even the white man, whose god walked and talked with him as friend to friend, cannot escape our common destiny. We may be brothers after all. We shall see."

ACKNOWLEDGMENTS

The authors would like to thank Pearl Means for her invaluable assistance in editing this book. We also thank John Crowther, who formatted the print edition.

14938233R00066

Printed in Poland
by Amazon Fulfillment
Poland Sp. z o.o., Wrocław